WHAT IS PSYCHOLOGY?

Connor Whiteley

Copyright © 2020 Connor Whiteley

All rights reserved.

https://www.subscribepage.com/psychologyboxset

ACKNOWLEDGMENTS
Thank you to all my wonderful readers as without your support I couldn't do what I love.

INTRODUCTION: WHY WRITE THIS BOOK?

Personally, I love psychology.

I love what is it, the science and the behaviour that psychology studies so after my Sixth Form or High School years. I decided to follow my passion for psychology as well as human behaviour further than this introductory education.

Resulting in me currently studying the very long degree of 'Psychology with Clinical Psychology with a Placement Year' at a university in the South East of England in the United Kingdom.

In other words, I study human behaviour at an English university with a few units specialising in mental disorders.

However, education isn't enough for me so I'm an author and after writing over 20 books, ten of these books being psychology books. I have decided to write this psychology book as an ultimate introduction to psychology.

As a result, whilst this book will NOT be an ultimate guide to the ins and outs of psychology because that's what the rest of my psychology books focus on.

This book will explain what psychology is and the many interesting areas of psychology as well as it will discuss sample topics from these areas using sample chapters from my other psychology books.

Who Is This Book For?

This book is for anyone who wants to learn about psychology as well as this book is for people who want to know about psychology but have no idea where to start.

I promise you this is the perfect starting point on your psychological journey of discovery…

CHAPTER 1: WHAT IS PSYCHOLOGY, WHAT IS PSYCHOLOGISTS DO AND WHY IS PSYCHOLOGY RELEVANT?

Personally, I think this is an odd question because when you answer this question to people they tend to think that psychology is only profiling on crime programs.

However, I hate to tell you that this is not the case, and to give you a bit of interesting context psychology comes from two Greek words. 'Psyche' meaning mind and soul as well as 'logos' meaning study.

Therefore, psychology literally means the study of the mind.

Nonetheless, as psychology has evolved over the past century and a bit the definition of psychology has changed.

For example, the current definition of

psychology according to the Oxford English Dictionary is: 'The Scientific study of the human mind and its function, especially in a given content'

In addition, I would love to stress that psychology is a science as everything in psychology is supported by data and findings from experiments and studies.

Whilst, I will fully admit that some psychology studies are better than other studies. All psychological facts are supported by data and subjected to psychological peers that review the study to see if the findings are good.

What Do Psychologists Do?

Everyone has their own reasons for reading about psychology. Like: I read psychology books because I'm interested, I'm doing a degree in psychology and I wish to become a Clinical Psychologist one day.

Even if you do not want to study psychology it's fine, you can keep reading, and psychology is good to know in any situation.

Although, if you do complete a degree and the other requirements then you can become a:

- Clinical Psychologist
- Educational Psychologist

- Forensic Psychologist
- Sport Psychologist
- Social Psychologist
- Occupational Psychology
- And many more…

<u>How Does Psychology Apply To You?</u>
Throughout this book and this series, we will be looking at psychological facts and research as well as psychology can affect us in a great number of ways. Such as:

- What factors increase the chance of us committing a crime?
- What causes relationships to form?
- How do hormones impact our behaviour?

In addition, there is a lot of psychological research out there in the world, meaning that you might want to go and investigate certain topics in more depth…

CHAPTER 2: APPROACHES IN PSYCHOLOGY

In psychology, there are many different approaches that people can take in order to investigate behaviour effectively.

<u>The Biological Approach:</u>

This approach to psychology and behaviour proposes that all behaviour is a result of biological processes.

Furthermore, this approach can be broken down into the following: The physiological approach proposed that all behaviour is linked to internal body parts. Like the brain and neurochemicals.

The nativist approach is a belief that all behaviour is inherited and passed from one generation to the next through our genes

Finally, the medical model proposes the idea that you can treat mental disorders like you would a physical disease due to the belief that every problem has a physical cause. For example, depression is caused by brain damage. (This is a fictional fact used to the demonstrate the medical model)

Biological Assumptions:

Additionally the biological approach has three basic assumptions that form the foundations for this approach to behaviour.

- Evolutionary inference- this is applying evolutionary theory by Charles Darwin in 1800s to psychology as psychologists use evolutionary Theory to explain how behaviour has changed over millions of years changed over time. Proposing that the human brain has changed because it was needed to adapt and survive.
- Localisation- we will explore this topic in more detail with the sample chapter in the next chapter, but localisation states that certain brain areas are associated with certain behaviours.
- Neurotransmitters- these are chemicals are that released by the brain in order to have certain effects on the body. For example, dopamine is a neurotransmitter that is responsible for the feeling of romantic love.

For more information on Biological Psychology, please check out [Biology Psychology.](#)

The Cognitive Approach:

This approach focuses on mental processes and how they affect behaviour.

We will explore Cognitive Psychology or the cognitive approach in Chapter 4.

Cognitive psychology has a few interesting assumptions about human behaviour as well.

For example, the cognitive approach believes that the human brain is like a computer and the brain is often compared to a computer. One example of this analogy is that long-term memory is like a computer hard drive.

Another assumption that cognitive psychology has is they believe that the human mind has internal mental processes that impact our behaviour.

Personally, I think that this assumption is fairly obvious as thinking is an internal mental process and that impacts on behaviour as we can make right or wrong decisions.

Finally, the cognitive approach believes in the idea of schemas. These are mental representations or frameworks in the human mind that influence the ways we encode, store and retrieval information.

For more information on cognitive psychology, please check out Cognitive Psychology.

The Behaviourist Approach:

our next approach focuses on the human mind being a black box so there's an input and there's a behavioural output.

For instance, if I was tapped on the shoulder then this information would be sent to my brain (the input) afterwards my brain would tell me to turn around. (the output)

Additionally, behaviourists believe that people behave because of life experience and it completely ignores cognitive and biological factors.

For example, a person could be rewarded for performances and behaviours or it could be punished. This life experience affects how they will behave in the future.

Another example would be that according to this approach depression would be caused by bullying only and it wouldn't consider genetic factors or cognitive/thinking style.

Assumptions:
In behaviourism, there are the following assumptions about human behaviour: humans are born like a blank slate meaning that humans learn from their

environment. This assumption follows the debate that human behaviour is based on nurture; how you bring up a child; compared to our genetics.

In addition, behaviourism has the assumption that humans learn through conditioning. For example, if you are punished after being 'naughty' then you have been conditioned (learnt) not to behave in that way again.

Finally, the behaviourists believe that humans, as well as animals, learn in similar ways. The main reason for this is probably because behaviourists and psychologists, in general, tend to animals in their experiments. Resulting in animal behaviour being compared to human behaviour often.

This can be seen throughout the series. For instance, if Romeo (2014)'s study on oxytocin and social bonding on dogs.

Psychodynamic Approach:

This approach proposes that human behaviour is as a result of the unconscious mind and emotions that are beyond our conscious awareness. For example, childhood memories that could be traumatic will influence our behaviour in the future.

Assumptions:

Firstly, the psychodynamic approach believes that the events of our childhood have a massive impact on our adult life.

Personally, I think this to be true as research has shown that trauma in childhood does affect your adult life.

A personal example would be the betrayals that I faced as a child greatly affects my ability to trust others as an adult.

Secondly, the psychodynamic approach believes in the unconscious mind. In other words, Freud believed that the mind is like an iceberg because most of the mind's working are underneath our conscious awareness.

In addition, Freud believed that the unconscious is responsible for most of our behaviour because we are driven by unconscious drives.

For example, we perform the behaviour of eating because the unconscious drive to survive and we need the energy from food to survive.

Lastly, the psychodynamic approach to behaviour proposes that the personality is made up of three parts that develop over time. For example:

- The Id develops at birth and this part of the personality is the unconscious mind that seeks to gain pleasurable no matter the cost.
- The Ego develops around the age of two years old and this part of the personality is the rational consciousness. This aspect must balance the need for pleasure and getting this pleasure in a socially acceptable way.
- The Superego develops around the age of four years old and this part encompasses the child's sense of right, wrong as well as the ideal self. This develops through identifying with one's parents or guardians, as well as the superego aims to civilise and perfect our behaviour.

Of course, there are issues with this approach to behaviour; like all approaches; but that is what the psychodynamic approach proposes.

The Positive Psychology Approach:

This next approach believes that psychology should study the positive aspects of human behaviour as well as positive human qualities, so people can live more fulfilled lives.

In addition, it's the belief that people want to enhance the experience of play, work and love that this approach is based on.

Assumptions:

Firstly, the positive approach acknowledges that humans have free will meaning that humans have a choice in their behaviour and how to act.

Whilst, this is debated in psychology. The focus of this section is to merely introduce what the approaches propose.

Secondly, the positive approach proposes that human goodness and positive emotions are authentic. I know that this wording may seem strange but in psychology, there's a focus on the negative emotions without acknowledging the positive emotions

In other words, this assumption means that psychology needs to acknowledge that happiness and other positive emotions are as important and serve our attention as much as negative emotions.

Finally, the positive approach looks at 'the good life' which are a set of factors that look at what makes a human life well-lived. The findings by Seligman (2003) show that the following lives are important, and they can flow in order:

- The pleasant life- in this life positivity comes from the active purse of positive emotions in relation to the past, present and future.
- The good life- positivity is reached by pursuing activities that positively engage with us as well as absorb us.

- The meaningful life- this approach to life means that we get enjoy from fulfilling a purpose that is greater than ourselves.

Personally, for the meaningful life is writing and being an author because it means that I can write these books and hopefully serve people in their quest to understand human behaviour.

CHAPTER 3: BIOLOGICAL PSYCHOLOGY

Building upon what we learned in the last chapter biological psychology is a very interesting area in my opinion because it goes into so much detail about why our biology impacts our behaviour.

Overall, biological psychology looks at our physical biological make-up in order to find out how our biology impacts our behaviour.

Some of these areas of study include:

- Localisation--this will be looked at in the sample chapter below.
- Neuroplasticity- this is how the brain changes or remaps itself because of environmental demands. (I love this topic)
- Hormones and Neurotransmitters- these are both neurochemicals that are secreted into the blood (hormones) or nervous system

(neurotransmitters) to influence our behaviour.

For example, the neurotransmitter serotonin is responsible for sleep and emotional regulation whereas the hormone oxytocin is responsible for social bonding.

- Evolution- this explains how our behaviour has evolved over time to help us to survive.
- Pheromones--these are chemical messages that transit information from one member of a species to another member.
- And many more interesting areas and all of these areas are explored in my book called Biological Psychology.

In order to give you a brief sample of what biological psychology is the example below using localisation, so I hope that you find this useful.

Personally, I find the localisation of Interest because some of the studies that look at that are writing and how it impacts our behaviour, I find amazing.

Note: This is a sample chapter from Biological Psychology.

Chapter 1- Localization:

The first stop on our journey to understand how biology can affect our behaviour is the theory of localisation.

Localisation is the theory that certain areas of the brain are responsible for certain psychological functions.

A possibly simpler way to think about it is that certain areas of a computer are responsible for its functions.

For example a hard drive storages information much the same way how the brain stores memories.

Furthermore, there are two types of localisation:

- Strict localisation which in its simplest terms means that one area of the brain is responsible for a psychological function.
- Weak localisation which is the idea that one area of the brain is dominant in a function, but other areas of the brain may take over its function as well.

We will explore these two ideas as we go along in this chapter.

Research into this area started over 150 years ago with our first case study.

Paul Broca (1861)

Broca was a French physician who treated a man for gangrene fever called: Lebrogne. By the age of 30, Lebrogne had lost the ability to speak and communicate.

However, all of his other functions were still in tac as when you tried to talk to him, he understood and tried to communicate back. Nevertheless, he could only say the word 'Tan' which he usually repeated twice.

His condition was named: Broca's aphasias- the loss of articulated speech.

When 'Tan' died aged 50 a brain autopsy discovered a lesion in his frontal left hemisphere of the brain.

If you wanted to be specific… it was in the posterior inferior frontal gyrus area. Now that's a mouthful!

After this discover Broca named the area of the brain after himself and concluded after studying another 25 patients that the Broca area was responsible for the forming of articulated speech.

Overall, this study supports the idea of strict localisation because it shows that if the Broca area is damaged that the function of speech is impaired as well.

Critical Thinking:

One aspect of the study that makes it good is that Broca studied another 25 people before drawing his conclusion. Meaning that he had a large sample size so his conclusion could be supported.

However, Broca preserved Tan's brain and 100 years later it was dissected, and the researchers found that the lesion wasn't as neat nor confined to the Broca area as previously thought.

So, it is possible that the Broca area isn't responsible for speech?

It is possible that another area of the brain that was affected by this lesion was, in fact, responsible for the forming of speech.

Further Support For Localisation:

Each of these lobes plays a key role in behaviour:

The Frontal Lobe- associated with executive functions. Like planning, decision making and speech.

The Occipital Lobe- associated with sight.

The Parietal Lobe- associated with the perception of stimuli.

The Temporal Lobe- associated with hearing and

memory.[1]

Lashley (1929)

On the other hand, not all functions of the brain are localised. One example that we'll look at now is memory.

In a typical experiment, he would train a rat to go through a maze to find a food pellet without an error.

Following this, he would remove a part of the brain. These removed sections would range from 10% to 50%.

The point of removing certain areas of the brain was that if memory was stored in one place then if you removed certain areas of the brain one at a time you would eventually find it.

The results of his experiment didn't support his theory that memory was localised. Therefore, he decided that it was because the amount of brain matter destroyed impacted memory and not the location. (known as the principle of mass action) and because one area of the brain could take over the function of another area of the brain. This is known of equipotentiality.

---

[1] https://www.thinkib.net/psychology/page/22420/localization-plasticity

Therefore, as Lashley couldn't find an area of the brain responsible for memory. This doesn't support the theory of localisation, and he proposed that memory is evenly spread out through the brain.

His theory is generally accepted today but memory is known not to be as uniformly and evenly spread out as Lashley thought.

Critically Thinking:

While Lashley did manage to prove that memory is not localised to one area of the brain. It begs the question and opens up the classic psychological debate of how far can we compare animals to humans as while we share a lot of our DNA with rats. As a result of physical differences and differences in our brain. Can this conclusion be accurately applied to humans?

Conclusion:

Personally, I think that we can agree that certain areas of the brain are localised to specific areas. While others are not.

What do you think?

Overall, localisation can affect behaviour because it demonstrates that certain areas of the brain are responsible for key behaviours that are important to humans. For example, the Broca area is responsible for articulated speech which is important for the survival of the species. The ability to communicate is one another.

Summary:

Localisation is the theory that certain areas of the brain are responsible for certain psychological functions.

Broca (1861) supports this theory as he found that the Broca area is responsible for articulated speech.

Whereas Lashley (1929) doesn't support the theory as it found that memory is localised.

After reading that short sample chapter on localisation I hope that you can start on the see that our biology has a clear effect on our behaviour and this is only the tip of the iceberg not to quote to the psychodynamic approach because biological psychology has a lot to offer.

However, it must be noted the biological approach to behaviour is not the only approach that can be taken and this is only one aspect of human behaviour. Let's move onto the next approach to human behaviour.

CHAPTER 4: COGNITIVE PSYCHOLOGY

Moving on from the biological approach to behaviour or biological psychology, we'll be looking at the cognitive approach to behaviour or cognitive psychology.

Personally, I find this approach to be very interesting and possibly a lot more interesting than biological psychology. As a result, this is a bit more of what people would typically call psychology because unlike the biological approach there isn't as much hard science to supports our findings and our claims.

Unless this does not make it a less interesting field or any less a science.

Overall, cognitive psychology is a subfield of psychology that specialises in mental processes. This will be briefly looked at in the approach section.

Consequently, building upon what we learnt in that section cognitive psychology looks at a lot of different topics within our mind to try and understand how our cognition/thinking affects our behaviour.

One example is in my book [Cognitive Psychology](#) we look at the following areas: memory, the reliability of memory, how memory works, thinking biases, how technology affects our thinking, emotion and memory, schemas and many more different and fascinating areas.

Below is a sample chapter from cognitive psychology and I hope you and I hope that you find useful as this teaches you about the reliability of memory because maybe memory isn't as reliable as you think.

On a quick personal note, I think the reliability of memory is an amazing topic because we all know from everyday life that memory is not always 100% reliable however this topic can give us an explanation to why and that is what I love about it.

Chapter 4: Reliability Of Memory

When I first learnt about what's contained in this chapter, I found it really interesting because I had noticed that memory was obviously faulty and people changed the memory from what actually happened, but I didn't know why or what it was called. Thus, when I learnt the why it was good to be able to explain to myself why other people's memories had changed so much.

Let's look deeper into this line of thinking. Let's say you're driving home and in reality, there was a car crash in front of you involving three cars. However, you remember there being four cars and 2 cyclists. Why?

Overall, there are many factors that could be the reason why like:

Post-event information- information about the event you're given after the event. This could be the reason because you overheard someone saying, "Thank god those two cyclists didn't get hit," it's a possibility.

Misleading questions- this is were a question suggests information that isn't entirely true. For example: "How many cars were involved? Four?"

Nevertheless, the main theory involved in the reliability of memory is reconstructive theory. It's suggested that memory in the LTM isn't a passive process that stays the same as when the information is encoded. In fact, it could be an active recreation of the event every time we replay the event in our mind.

Additionally, the theory recognises that information that we encode during the event and after the event can; at least overtime; merge together to form a new memory to the point where we can't tell them apart anymore.

Hence, why we remember 4 cars instead of 3.

Loftus and Pickerel (1995):

This study suggests another reason why memory isn't reliability.

They asked family and friends about 3 childhood memories of the participants and if they had ever been lost in the mall. If the answer was yes, they weren't accepted into the study.

Then they sent a questionnaire through the post containing the 3 memories and the lost in the mall memory.

They were asked to write as much as they could about the memory and rate how confident they were about the memory.

The results showed that 25% of people did believe the lost in the mall memory however they rated it as their least confident memory.

Overall, showing that memory can be unreliability as false memories can be created.

Critically Thinking:

While the study shows that false memories can be created. It was only 25% of people and since it was done at home. The subject could have conferred with others.

Yuille and Cutshall (1986):

Although, memory can be reliable as demonstrated in this study where: 4 months after a gun store robbery were the owner was shot twice and killed. The researchers contacted the 21 witnesses and 13 of them signed up for the study.

They were asked to recall what happened during the robbery, then half of them were asked: did you see a blue panel on the getaway car? When it was yellow.

Then the other half was asked: did you were a broken headlight on the getaway car? When it wasn't.

Plus, they were asked were they afraid?

Results showed that they were 79%-84% accurate when compared to old police reports.

10 out of 13 recalled correctly the answer to their leading question.

While they weren't afraid, they did experience an Adrenaline rush.

Critically Thinking:

The study has high ecological validity as this was a study involving a real event.

But as it was a one-off the results are unreproducible and unrepeatable. Although, the researchers could test other similar events to see if the results could be simpler.

Summary:

The main reason why memory can be unreliable is because of reconstructive theory.

Loftus and Pickerel (1995) shows our memory can be unreliable because of false memories.

Whereas Yuille and Cutshall (1995) shows us that memory can be reliable as the witnesses were 79%-84% correct when compared to police reports.

After reading this chapter, I hope that you are beginning to understand that psychology covers a lot of different perspectives and behaviours.

Now we'll be moving onto our last main approaches of psychology. That's called: sociocultural psychology that I personally love.

For more information on Cognitive Psychology,

please check out my book Cognitive Psychology.

CHAPTER 5: SOCIOCULTURAL PSYCHOLOGY

Sociocultural psychology is our last approach that we're going to look at and it's one of my favourites.

One of the reasons for this is because when I was taught this approach during sixth form or High School we were taught by an anthropologist and, in essence, this is the study of culture and sociocultural processes. Resulting in that having the perfect person to teach us and she gave us an incredible insight that is still present within me today.

Overall sociocultural psychology is the combination and is a subfield of social psychology. Meaning social psychology; this is the psychology of group processes and the individual; as well as cultural psychology. This looks at how culture affects our behaviour.

Personally, I love social and cultural psychology-

and sociocultural psychology is the perfect intersection for the types of psychology. I love to understand why people behave the way they do in groups as well as I love to know about different cultures and how these different cultures that we are exposed to impacts our behaviour.

Sociocultural psychology covers the following aspects of human behaviour:

- Social influence- this looks at topics like obedience, the peer pressure as well as how groups influence their members.
- The social group- this topic looks at how social groups are formed and what is a group as it's not as simple as you would think.
- Social cognitive Theory- this investigates how we learn by watching others and its consequences.
- Social identity Theory- this theory looks at intergroup conflict and it has six main claims about groups and their identities.
- Globalisation- personally this is a very interesting area that looks at how globalisation; the world becoming more interconnected; impacts our behaviour.
- Cultural dimensions- going into cultural psychology this topic looks on the difference between cultures in their values, belief as well as attitudes.

- Stereotypes- the area of social psychology that looks at how stereotypes form and their impact on human behaviour.
- And many, many more

This sample chapter is an absolute classic for social psychology as this looks at the social group. This is a very interesting area that I hope that you enjoy.

In my opinion, the social group is one of my favourite areas of social psychology. Due to I believe that this topic is proper social psychology and as a human being it is great to see the psychology behind group processes because after being in various social groups in my life. I love to be able to understand why people behave the way they do because sometimes people are very strange.

This is an extract from Sociocultural Psychology Second Edition.

The Social Group:

Groups are central to human existence; without them, we can't survive and our ancestors showed us the power of these social groups. As a result, we were able to build vast cities and empires because we formed groups.

For example, the Romans joined together and started the roman empire as well as the British united to start the British Empire and we managed to conquer a third of the world, but that was a very long time ago.

In addition, groups influence who we are and how we live.

What Is A Group?

This is not a simple question because a group can be large or small, structured or unstructured, specific or general, physically close or scattered (Deaux et al, 2995) as well as group can perhaps a feeling of common fate (Lewis, 1948)

For example, I can feel that I am a part of the psychology student group but this group in itself is massive as it's spread national and international borders.

Another example is that I am a student and a part of the student group. This group is close to me at the university yet this group has many subgroups as well. For example, the successful and unsuccessful students, the students doing different degrees as well as the party-loving students and the non-partying students.

According to Johnson and Johnson (1987), these are the essential features of a group: interaction, people need to perceive the self as part of the group, groups need to be interdependent, they need to have a common goal, structure of norms or rules as well as the members need to influence each other, and the group need to have a joint association to satisfy a need.

Referring to my personal examples, back in secondary school or middle school. I was a part of the Warhammer 40,000 wargaming club. As a group we had a common goal; this was to play Warhammer 40,000, and we had interaction.

However, we weren't interdependent yet we were still a group so these essential features aren't universal or cannot apply to all groups.

Two more ideas of a group definition are from Tajfel (1981) is: 'two or more individuals… perceive themselves to be members of the social category' and 'Us versus them' from Turner (1982)

Social Identity Theorists:

According to Social Identity Theorists, as discussed in a previous chapter, they define a group as two more people who themselves and are recognised by others as groups and have a sense of 'us' which can be compared to 'them' formations of groups.

This definition works as a general definition as well.

In other words, social identity theorists believe

that a group is made up of two or more people and the important part of the group is that the members of this group and non-member must see this group as a group. Furthermore, the theorists state that the group has a concept of ingroup and outgroup, as discussed in the Social Identity chapter.

Group Formation:

According to Tuckerman (1965), there are 5 stages of group formation.

Forming is the first stage and it involves coming together, accepting each other, avoiding conflict and working out the purpose and roles of the group.

Secondly, you have the storming phase. This is where you address issues within the group. There's usually some intergroup conflict but this conflict can be supported in harmony.

After the storming stage, you have the norming stage. In this stage, the group focuses on listening, supporting and being flexible to other group members. In addition, the group usually has a common identity and a purpose by this stage.

The last two stages are the performing stage. This is where the group is very task orientated as well as adjoining is the last stage. This is when the task is completed, and the group disengages.

Group Socialisation:

Group socialisation is the process of the group and its member coming together and meeting each other's needs over time.

Moreover, the group and each individual member of the group are constantly evaluating each other to see if the group is right for them.

When it comes to group socialization, Moreland and Levine (1982) have proposed these five stages:

Firstly, a person is a prospective member of a group and they are investigating whether the group is right for them.

Afterwards, the member joins the group and starts to socialise with the group. This is when they become part of the group. The stage is being a marginal member.

Next, the member goes through the maintenance stage. This is where they are a full member and only need to maintain their standing or position in the group.

However, if a group member doesn't maintain their group membership then they may need to go through reconciliation. Where they are earning the trust of the group back and learning how to be a full member again.

On the other hand, if they fail in resocialization then they can quit the group entirely. This stage is called remembrance.

Interestingly, people being a part of a group can still be important years after they left the group. We will come back to this later in the chapter.

In addition, group socialisation often involves initiation rites and 'people accept negative outcomes due to cognitive dissonance' (Festinger, 1967) and as a result, they put the group in higher esteem to combat dissonance.

Interestingly, even a person is subjected to an extremely humiliating initiation rite. It can make that person want to be a part of that group even more.

One reason for this behaviour would be that the individual wants to make sure that the act of humiliation wasn't done in vain.

Overall, groups benefit from socialisation and there's a range of socialisation outcomes that describe how the group member feel about how they function. Most commonly it is group coherence.

Forces Within A Group:

There are a lot of forces within a group and all these different forces influence the group and shape the group into what the world sees.

According to Festinger et al (1950), the forces within a group are:

The attractiveness of group members and the group. This describes the forces that make you like the group.

Social interaction goals- does the amount of social interaction in the group meet what you're looking for.

Individual goals- does the group help you to meet your goals.

Individual goals interdependent with group

Coherence- is the group united.

Behaviour- does your behaviour adhere to the standards of the group.

<u>Norms:</u>

In my opinion, group norms are very interesting because all groups have them as well as each group has its own unique set of norms.

For example, in the author community, the norms are: produce high-quality work, engage with readers and be human.

Norms can be defined as the individual set of behaviour and attitudes that determine, organise and defines groups from another group.

These norms can be formal or informal but all norms regardless of the group help to regulate and guide the group's behaviour.

Furthermore, norms provide us with a frame of reference so we know how to behave in a certain group and some norms are universal, as well as some vary across cultures

Ultimately, norms can guide our behaviour in a group, but they can change attitudes and behaviour as well. Typically, this happens when we desire to be part of a certain group.

Why Do Norms Work?

Norms work for several reasons. For example, groups often encourage them, so we quickly learn the group's norms during socialisation as well as we often internalise them.

As a result, whenever we are with the group, we remember the norms and the norms become activated.

Overall, social norms act as action heuristics to make life easier.

Are Norms Good At The Group Level?

In my opinion and the research has shown that the answer is yes because Coch and French (1948) found that by permitting groups to form their own norms. They increased in the group's effectiveness because the group decided how they wanted to work.

Roles:

In this section, we're going to get into the tricky subject of social roles.

On a personal note, I don't believe in social roles. For example, I don't believe in women should be housewives and men have to be the breadwinner of the family.

Social roles are shared exceptions of how people in groups are supposed to behave. For example, in my Warhammer 40,000 club, I oversaw the group, so my social role was that of the leader.

A positive about social roles is that groups with set roles tend to be more satisfied and performed better (Barley and Beckly, 2004)

Roles can sometimes make the group lose sight of right and wrong. Especially, when these social roles seem illegitimate or arbitrary. Like: gender.

Gender Roles:

Gender roles can cause conflict as well as they can change who we are. As supported by Twenge (2001) who tracked women's social status between 1931-1993 and compared the findings with women's ratings of their own assertiveness.

The results showed that the pattern followed trends in women's social status. Meaning that social roles are linked to status.

Status:

In society and within any group different social role has different statuses as some roles are valued more than others. For example, the Head of State compared to a blue-collar worker.

These differences in status reflect social comparison within groups. (Festinger, 1954) and people often legitimise status differ. For example, men legitimising the historical and still present gender inequality.

Yet interestingly people can support systems that are unfair to them personally. (Jost and Banaji, 2004) for instance, my lecturer used the example of a poor woman with three children living in social housing. You would probably find that that woman supports the government and the system that isn't helping her get out of poverty.

Social Creativity:

Sometimes the social groups we are a part of do negative things or they conduct themselves in a way that makes our esteem for the group decrease.

This happened to me a few years ago with scouting as some of the things that were going on in scouting made me dislike the group.

However, humans tend to prefer to maintain esteem for a group. Especially, when the group is important to us. Like how scouting was important for me.

Therefore, people engage in social creativity to help improve their esteem for a group.

Social creativity is the strategies that a person uses to improve and maintain their esteem for a group.

One strategy that people can use is focusing on another dimension. (Tajfel and Turner, 1979)

Such as We are a poor country but we are good at sports.

Deviants:

These types of people are marginal group members and they are generally disliked because they make it more difficult to hold the group in high esteem. Additionally, they threaten the positive image of the ingroup. (Marques et al, 2001)

For example, if a few members of the church decide to start attacking non-Christians then these deviants most certainly threaten the positive image of Christianity.

On the other hand, deviants can be good for the group because they can point out things that are wrong with the group so they can be improved. (Parker, 2008, 2010)

Group Sensitivity:

Humans can be sensitive people and the Intergroup sensitivity effect (Homer et al 2002) is when we are more likely to accept criticism if it's from the ingroup.

In my opinion, this is relatively true as I am more likely to accept criticism about a study if it's another psychology student or someone in the field of psychology compared to someone who isn't.

Imposters:

This is a new but interesting area of research that examines how imposters affect the social group and Jetten et al (2005) presented vegetarians with meat eaters and when one of the vegetarian group members was caught eating meat. The group dealt with them harsher than the outgroup members.

Schism:

This is when the group breaks off and these smaller groups form their own subgroups.

In addition, subgroups can engage in cross-cutting. In essence, this is when these subgroups include and mix with other people that aren't apart of the larger group.

The easier example of crosscutting would be if a subgroup of the UK Conservative Political Party decided to include members of a subgroup of the Labour Party into their numbers.

What Do Groups Do For Us?

Groups do a lot for our mental health as well as they do a lot for us. Including:

They help us with interdependence.

You give us affiliation, support and similarity.

We can achieve more in a group than alone. (Thibaut and Kelley, 1959)

Terror management- people look for structure in life to confront the terror of death (Greenberg et al, 1966)

They provide us with a social identity.

Positive consequences for the self

They give us the motivation to protect the group

Optimal Distinctiveness:

It is natural for humans to want to distinguish themselves from others as well as to make themselves feel special and this is what groups can do us. (Brewer, 1991)

For example, I want to be distinguished in the job market from the rest of my group. In this case, my group is a psychology graduate. Therefore, I want to distinguish myself my writing books and being an author.

Ostracism And Social Exclusion:

When people are excluded from things people tend to feel sad, angry and psychologically distressed. I know this from experience.

Interestingly, it hurts us even when we don't belong to the group that excludes us. (Gonsaikrale and Williams, 2007) as well as this mental pain has demonstrated in neuroscience studies to reassemble real physical real.

Resembles pain in neuroscience studies

I hope that you enjoyed the sample chapter because I know that I loved writing and learning about it during my university lectures.

Now we have looked at the various approaches you can take in psychology, we are now going to look at the different topics in psychology that I have other books on. These other topics I truly hope that you enjoy and find as interesting as I do- our first topic is Abnormal Psychology also known as Clinical Psychology.

If you want to learn more information on Social and cultural psychology then please check out, Sociocultural Psychology 2nd Edition.

CHAPTER 6: ABNORMAL PSYCHOLOGY

This area of psychology is honestly my favourite subfield of psychology because I love abnormalities or strange things. As a result, all humans are strange to extremely varying degrees as normality is merely a social construct.

Can you define normal behaviour?

However, going back to abnormal psychology or clinical psychology. This area focuses on the causes and treatment of mental disorders. For example, depression, psychosis, eating disorders and Autism Spectrum disorders.

In fact, this area of psychology builds on the approaches of psychology because each approach helps us to understand why a disorder develops and how to treat it.

For Example, the biological approach helps us to understand depression because the serotonin hypothesis starts that depression is caused by an imbalance of the neurotransmitter serotonin. Meaning that to treat depression we need to use drugs that restore this balance.

Nonetheless, the biological approach is only one perspective to take for the causes of depression. Below is another perspective is taken from my book [Abnormal Psychology.](#)

Chapter 3: Cognitive Explanation

Moving to our next point of interest is how can our mental processes affect our chance of developing MDD.

Now the main theory of depression used for this type of explanation is: Beck (1967) and the theory states that cognition (mental processes) is the main reason behind depression and focuses on the impact that a change in automatic thoughts can have on behaviour. The theory focuses on:

The cognitive triad- negative beliefs about the self, the world and the future. These influence the automatic thoughts to be pessimistic.

Negative schema- the negative beliefs about themselves become generalize and people start to think negatively about everything that happens to them.

Faulty thinking patterns- people think and make illogical conclusions because of how they process information is biased.

Personally, I do quite like the theory because if you know someone with depression as I did then you can see some of this theory out to light.

In addition, I think that it's a reasonably easy theory to follow.

But let's put this theory into context, according to this theory a depression is caused by:

(I know some the examples are poor)

The cognitive triad- this can be demonstrated when a depressed person says things. Like: "I'm useless," or "Oh the world is falling apart so what's the point of living?"

Negative schemas- as demonstrated by this: "Oh I failed in art so I'm never to pass any subjects, go to university and I'm just going to be a failure in life,"

Faulty thinking patterns- this could be shown in a setting when researching a holiday to the most beautiful place ever and there was a 0.5% chance of a terror attack. "Oh no, I can't go there I'm going to die,"

While that last example wasn't the best. It shows how illogical conclusions can be made because of a bias towards the negative.

Supporting Studies:

This first study shows how having a negative thinking style can affect depression.

Alloy, Abramson and Francis (1999):

Quasi-experiment and longitudinal study for 5.5 years with a questionnaire and structured interviews.

Freshmen were given a questionnaire to determine their cognitive style and they were split into two groups based on the results.

High risk; the negative cognitive style; believed that negative life events were cataphoric and the results meant that they were flawed and worthless.

During the first 2.5 years, high-risk people were more likely to develop symptoms of major depression. (17% versus 1%)

High-risk people were more likely to have suicidal thoughts and behaviour (28% versus 13%)

In conclusion, negative cognitive style can lead to the development of major depression.

Critically Thinking:

This study was a longitudinal study, so this allowed the researchers to show the effects of a negative thinking style over time.

Yet it was a quasi-experiment without a clear independent variable and the dependent variable, so it can't be said if the study has strong internal validity; does the study measure what it intended to; as it wasn't clear what the study was measuring.

Caseras et al (2007):

Quasi-experiment with eye-tracking technology

Using the Beck Depression Inventory, the subjects were assessed for depressive symptoms and then split into two groups. Depressed and non-depressed.

Then the subjects were shown 32 pictures paired with a positive, neutral and negative stimuli and each picture was shown for 3 seconds.

Using eye-tracking technology, the researchers measured what stimuli the subject first focused on and how long they focused on it before they switched to another stimulus.

Results showed that depressed people have an attention bias for the negative stimuli because once they looked at the negative stimuli, they found it hard to move onto another stimulus.

Critically Thinking:

The study used a large sample bias so the findings can be applied to large groups of people as we know that this trend of behaviour is shown by a number of people.

However, this is a reductionist way of thinking. A way of thinking that tries to find a single cause for depression without thinking of other factors and more holistic research that considers biological, cognitive and social factors of depression needs to be done.

Summary:

Beck (1967) theory focuses on the cognitive triad, negative schemas and faulty thinking processes.

Alloy, Abramson and Francis (1999) shows how a negative thinking style can lead to depression.

Caseras et al (2007) found that depressed people have an attention bias to negative stimuli.

As you can see from this half of the chapter, depression isn't caused by one factor only. In fact, it's caused by a combination of biological, cognitive and social factors.

For more information on the causes and

treatment of depression, please check out Abnormal psychology.

Global Mental Health and Culture:

Furthermore, culture plays a massive role in the development of depression because our culture impacts how depression is perceived by society as well as how it's treated.

Personally, I love this area of psychology truly because I love culture and mental disorders, so this global mental health book was perfect to write.

The best example is in the sample chapter below:

Moving onto our first exploration, in this chapter, we'll be examining how culture impacts mental health in terms of treatment and beliefs in Asia. Focusing on Japan and China.

Japan:

As you will see as we look in this chapter, the Japanese approach to mental health couldn't be more different from the western approach.

One of the reasons for this is because depression in Japan isn't seen as a mental health disorder.

As a result of in Japan, the depressed personality type is admired and aspired. Which is radically different from the west as in the west we frown upon the depressed personality and we certainly don't aspire to it.

Therefore, we must think about why is it aspired to. While I'll fully admit that my research didn't find a reason why. One reason that could explain this admiration I'll explain in a moment after we look at mental health in Japan in more depth.

In Japanese culture, sadness, grief and depression are seen as well as accepted as an everyday part of life.

Moreover, based on Buddhist traditions, personal difficulties and by extension depression is seen as character building.

Consequently, could this admiration towards the depressed personality type be as a result of people seeing depression as the ultimate way to build character and people aspire to be depressed so that they can go on this unique character-building journey, to come out with a strong character?

It's logical reasoning.

Another unique or different approach to mental health in Japan compared to the west is that historically suicide isn't linked to mental health.

Due to in Japanese culture suicide has a tradition that is linked to honour as well as dedication.

Many historical Japanese figures have performed

suicide to avoid bringing shame or dishonour to their families, with the thinking being that if they die; the 'dishonourable' member of the family; then with the dead then honour is restored to the family. Like how honour killing work in the middle east or western crime families.

Examples of Japanese figures performing suicide are Samurai warriors and kamikaze pilots.

Although, the most interesting piece of this is that Japanese therapists, psychologists and psychiatrists don't see a link between suicide and mental health.

Nevertheless, Japan is starting to change very slowly to become more westernised because if you compare depression symptoms before and after westernisation then you would find that after westernisation depression symptoms are becoming like the symptoms of depression that show up in western cultures.

As symptoms for disorders do differ sometimes a lot between cultures.

Additionally, here are some surprising statistics about mental health in Japan.

6.6% of the population has met the standards for western cultures to state that the Japanese have depression.

Japan has 26 suicide a year per 100,000 people. Compared to only 13 suicides per year per 100,000 in the USA.

Prozac; an antidepressant; sells well in Japan but not as much as in other countries in the world.

A Ministry of Health survey demonstrates that there's an increase in the number of children accessing mental health services. From 95,000 in 2002 to 148,000 in 2008.

Overall, suggesting that Japan does have a mental health problem as shown by its high suicide rate and the fact that Prozac sells well in Japan. Suggesting that a high number of people are taking in to deal with everyday life.

On the other hand, it's selling better in other countries suggesting that Japan has less of a mental health problem than other countries or more people prefer eastern methods of treatment compared to the west.

Returning to the point raised in the previous chapter about there are exceptions to the statement that there's a lack of reliable studies to examine the effectiveness of indigenous therapy.

Morita therapy is a therapy that is rooted in the fundamental beliefs as well as values of the Japanese culture. These values and beliefs include:

Emotions are natural responses to our life circumstances, and humans don't need to try to "fix" or "change" them.

Dogmatic thinking- this thinking is that perfectionism in conjunction with high demands of the self, inhibit recovery and only when we are liberated from self-centeredness can we recover.

In recovery, it's essential that are we left alone and resting instead of talking about our problems.

This type of Japanese therapy typically begins with a rest period before counselling begins. Although compared to counselling in the west, this counselling focuses on changing one's view toward the larger community instead of the self.

The therapy asks the patient to practise mindfulness through meditation as well.

Finally, the focus of the therapy is healing, not the origins of the disorder.

Applying This To Western Treatment:

Backing away from the theory, we can start to see the differences between this Japanese approach to treatment and the western methods of treatment.

As a result of in the west; at least in my experience; we don't believe or focus on mindfulness but in Japan, they believe that mindfulness is essential to recovery.

Another key difference between the western and Japanese approach is that in western treatment we focus on the origins of the disorder. Such as we focus on the biological, cognitive or social factors that could have caused the disorder. One way of doing this could be identifying any bad relationships in your life that could be causing your depression and encouraging you to change these relationships to become more positive or getting rid of these negative relationships completely.

Whereas the Japanese approach focuses on healing and moving on from the disorder.

Both I believe has its merits and drawbacks. For example, the western approach is good as it focuses on the causes of the disorder so these causes can be removed as a way towards recovery.

However, this method can seem a little too focused on negative and why as well as it could take a very, very long time to find all the factors or causes of depression in a person's life.

On the other hand, the Japanese approach is good because it focuses on recovery so the patient can focus on moving and improving without having to spend hours dissecting painful parts of their life searching for things that could be causing depression.

Although the Japanese approach could be negative as it doesn't focus on the causes of the disorder and if these factors that are causing depression; like bad relationships, abuse and drug problems; are still in the person's life then there's a high chance of a relapse into depression.

Consequently, is it possible that the Japanese approach could be used to inform western treatment and improve it?

I strongly believe the answer is yes- because the Japanese approach works for Japan and its citizens. Therefore, I believe that if the western and Japanese approach hybridized to form a new type of treatment. Where the therapy focuses on origins and recovery then western treatment could be improved as we are focusing on the positive of recovery while finding the causes of depression and getting rid of them as well.

A study supporting the effectiveness of Japanese treatment is outlined below:

Ando et al (2009)

Researchers wanted to investigate the effect of mindfulness-based meditation therapy on Japanese patients who were suffering from anxiety and depression.

In total there were 28 patients that participated in two sessions of the therapy.

The patients were instructed to practice at home in-between sessions. The study used a pre-test / post-test design.

The patients completed questionnaires before as well as after the treatment.

Results showed that anxiety and depression levels decreased significantly. The researchers argue that a sense of spiritual wellbeing is what resulted in lower levels of both anxiety and depression.

Overall, supporting the idea that the Japanese approach that focuses on mindfulness is an effective treatment.

<u>China:</u>

China is another country of interest when it comes to mental health because China has its own classification system for health disorders as discussed in chapter 1 and inside the classification system that are many disorders that are unique to Chinese culture.

Such as Pa-Leng which is an extreme fear of the cold. This disorder seems to be unique to China as well as there are many other disorders that are unique to certain cultures. Hence, empathising the power of culture in mental health.

However, another reason China is of interest to this book is as a result of the mental health strain that is experienced by a lot of the Chinese population as it's suicide rate is reasonably high at 22.23 people per 100,00 because of the poor working conditions and other factors. Especially, with their being famous cases of mass suicides at Apple's Chinese Manufacture FOXCONN.

Source: www.asiaone.com/health/chinas-suicide-rate-among-highest-world *and* www.telegraph.co.uk

Referring Back To Indigenous Therapies:

Another integral part of indigenous therapies is spirituality or religious practices.

For instance: as part of the therapy in Malaysia some of the techniques include: setting aside time for pray and focusing on verses of the Koran that focus on "worry"

Whereas, with Chinese patients verses from Taoist writings that focus on the following main principles: restricting selfish desires, learning how to be content, and learning to let go, are read by the patient followed by a reflection.

This approach is known as Chinese Taoist cognitive psychotherapy (CTCP).

Zhang et al (2002)

Researchers carried out a study to test the effectiveness of CTCP.

In their study, 143 Chinese patients with Generalized Anxiety Disorder (GAD) were randomly assigned to one of three treatment groups: CTCP only, anti-anxiety drugs only, or a combination of the two.

The patients were evaluated before the study then after one month of their treatment and then again after six months of treatment.

Results showed that people on the anti-depressants showed better results than the CTCP group after one month.

Nevertheless, after six months those patients in the CTCP group had a greater reduction of symptoms.

Finally, people in the combined treatment group had the greatest symptom reduction with a low chance of relapse.

Overall, the researchers found that CTCP helped patients to reduce perfectionism as well as improve their coping skills. While the treatment was slower, the treatment appears to be more successful than drug treatment.

The results of this study are supported by other western studies that show that psychotherapy can be more effective in the long term for treating depression.

Please refer to Abnormal Psychology for a more in-depth look at the effectiveness of psychotherapies for treating depression.

Barriers To Treatment:

This next section truly shows how culture can negatively impact treatment or rather the ability for people to get treatment as a result of cultural factors.

A report by Leong and Kalibatseva (2011) outlines the key barriers for Chinese Americans for getting treatment.

Cognitive Barriers:

This type of barrier refers to the way in which people think about treatment and this is influenced by their culture.

It's a common belief in several ethnic minorities such as Asian, Hispanic, and African Americans that a mental health problem can be treated or overcome through willpower and endurance of hardship without complaint. Instead of going to a profession for treatment.

Some research has indicated that Asian

Americans are more likely than Caucasian Americans to believe that mental health was enhanced by exercising self-control.

Affective Barriers:

Many collectivistic cultures; cultures that tend to focus on the needs of the group instead of focusing on their own needs; avoid getting professional help in order to avoid the stigma as well as the shame of mental illness that is attached to mental health.

The main reason for this as we have previously mentioned in the Japanese section, it that the family's name is very important to collectivistic cultures and people don't want to bring shame or dishonour to their name because of their 'perceived weakness' or the fact that they are experiencing psychological difficulties and because of this people don't seek out professional help- so they can protect their family's reputation.

Sociocultural Barriers:

The report highlights many sociocultural barriers as well. For instance:

Disclosing personal problems or family dysfunctions to a stranger. This is highly discouraged in collectivistic cultures.

Lack of awareness or knowledge about available

services.

Mental health services could be unaffordable to people.

Patients may not have time to receive care as they need to work multiple jobs or take care of family members.

Patients could have low English proficiency of immigrants

There's a scarcity of bicultural and bilingual mental health professionals

Overall, Chinese culture has a massive impact on mental health from the increased strain on its citizens' mental health to its unique disorders. That I would encourage you to go and research for yourself. It's actually a fun activity to do.

In addition, the Chinese culture has a massive impact on treatment from china's specialized type of psychotherapy to the cultural barriers that prevent people from seeking professional help. It's futile to say that culture doesn't impact treatment.

In the book, [A Guide to Mental Health and Treatment: A Global Look at Depression](). We need explore other cultures and how they treat depression. For example, we look at African and Europe as well as we compare countries within each continent to truly show you the scope of culture impacting mental health.

CHAPTER 7: PSYCHOLOGY OF HUMAN RELATIONSHIPS

What causes human relationships to form?

What types of attraction and love are there?

How do relationships breakdown?

These questions are at the core of the psychology of human relationships investigates and all of these questions are very important in understanding human behaviour because if we don't understand how relationships form then as humans we are missing out on a lot of valuable knowledge. As a result, human relationships are essential to the human experience.

Now I will fully admit that the psychology of human relationships sometimes has something to be desired in terms of good research because some studies are interesting and others are done terribly or they lack ecological validity. This is how you can generalise the findings to the real world.

Nonetheless, I go into this issue in a lot more detail in my book is [The Psychology of Human Relationships.](#)

Going back to the approaches that you can take in psychology. The psychology of human relationships builds upon these approaches in a lot of depth.

For example, the biological approach to behaviour studies how our biology causes human relationships to form. Some examples of this include hormones and neurotransmitters as well as physical attractiveness.

The cognitive approach to behaviour looks at how our mental processes form human relationships. In addition, in this approach, there are two main theories. The Matching Principles and the Similarity-Attraction hypothesis.

Finally, the sociocultural approach to behaviour investigates how social Factors cause relationships to form. For example, social proof.

The psychology of human relationships is an extremely interesting area because it's great to attempt to apply science to the phenomena of love.

On the other hand, this isn't easy to do because 'what is love?' as most feelings of love are nothing more than chemical reactions in the brain. In addition, how do you apply science to love or feeling as you can't measure feelings directly?

Below is a sample chapter that aims to explore this further it was taken from my book the Psychology Of Human Relationships 2nd Edition.

Chapter 3: The Cognitive Explanations For The Formation Of Human Relationships

Now that we understand how our biology can cause us to feel attraction for someone or form other relationships. We can start to look at the psychological or mental reasons why we find people attractive as well as form other types of relationships.

In the cognitive realm of relationships, there are two main theories for relationships.

The first theory that we'll look at is the similarity-attraction hypothesis. This states that people form a relationship because they are similar to one another.

For example, think about your friend and you'll probably find that you're friends with them because you have things in common with them. Such as music preference, common interest and TV interests.

One personal example is that I and one of my friends have many common interests that are the foundation of our friendship. Such as scouting, sailing, opinions/attitudes and many more…

A study that supports this hypothesis is:

Byrne (1961):

Subjects were asked to rate a number of issues on their importance. Ranging from western films to premarital sex to music.

Then two weeks later they were shown a fake questionnaire. It was fake so one of four results could happen. Same on the important issues, same on the unimportant issues, opposite to the subject completely and the same as the subject on all issues.

Then they were asked to rate the attractiveness of the stranger based on their answers.

Results showed that more positive ratings were associated with a similar attitude as well as associated with similarity in important issues.

Critical Thinking:

The study has strong internal validity; they measured what they intended to measure; because the study effectively showed that attraction to the stranger was because they had more in common with them. This supports the hypothesis.

However, this study has low ecological validity; can you apply the findings to the real world; because in the real world nobody meets people and rates them on the basis of a questionnaire. Even people on dating websites tend to be shown pictures and other information that impacts on their rating of attractiveness.

Consequently, to improve the experiment another research method could be used to support the findings and add creditability to the study. For example, interviews to see if their ratings were down to similarities or another reason.

Matching Hypothesis:

The next major cognitive theory for the formation of personal relationships is the matching hypothesis.

This hypothesis states that we are more likely to be attracted to someone who is equally socially desirable.

One way to think about this hypothesis is that your current or past partner according to the hypothesis is about the same as you in terms of how socially desirable they are.

For example, a popular person would date a popular person, as well as a person of average attractiveness, would date an equally average person.

And so on…

Although, people can compensate for a potential difference by making up for this difference in other areas. For instance:

- Wealth
- Sense of humour
- Good social care

This makes perfect sense I think because in terms of social desirability a person that I wanted to date in the past was different, but we would have made up for it through other factors. Such as we both matched our sense of humour and a lot of our interests matched, so that's another way to think about it.

The matching hypothesis/ principle can be done through asset matching as well.

This is where you are looking to match what you have with someone else and one method of doing this asset matching is through advertising. Such as attractive 28-year old seeking professional man.

I know it's not the social norm but it happens.

A study that supports the hypothesis is:

Berscheid et al (1971):

Subjects were split into High Probability of rejection and low POR

High POR got to meet their dates before the dance to either reject or accept them.

Low POR was told that their dates agreed to go with whoever was chosen for them by the computer programme.

Results showed that attractive subjects choose equally popular and attractive dates compared to High POR who choose more unattractive dates.

As this was not different in the two groups increasing fear of rejection doesn't affect the choosing stagey.

In conclusion, the matching principle may be a determinant of initial contact but not of maintaining already established relationships.

Critical Thinking:

A positive of this study is that it can be reproduced therefore future studies can repeat the experiment to test the results. This is positive because it adds creditability to the study if the results are the same or similar.

On the other hand, this study has low temporal

validity; how time affects the results; because in this modern age of online dating and the crazy world of dating. It's possible that the results would be different as the computer programmes that had chosen the dates for the two groups could be more reliable or choose different dates for the two groups. Using more modern programmes to calculate the best match for the person.

Emotion:

Rather unsurprisingly emotion is something that is important for all human relationships and maybe it's not love. Nonetheless, emotion will be involved to some degree or another as well as positive feelings lead to positive evaluation and vice versa. (Bryne, 1977)

Meaning that if you have positive feelings towards someone then this will lead to evaluating someone else as positive.

Like, I had positive feelings about a person at school and after talking to them. This leads me to evaluate them in a positive manner. Increasingly the likelihood of talking to them again and forming a friendship. This friendship did happen.

Of course, when I discuss positive evaluations nobody actually sits there and thinks "Right let's make a list of the pros and cons of that person I met…

okay there are more pros than cons so I'll see them again'

I mean that we evaluate them both unconsciously and conscious even if it is only a quick thought. Like: when you think "God that conversation was long" or "Wow she's was interesting I think I'll definitely talk to her again"

Emotion or feelings towards someone can be direct; so you could possibly feel your attraction because of their physical appearance; or indirectly. For example, your feelings are not caused by that person.

An example of this emotional directionality from psychology research is Dutton and Aron (1974) were they got participants to walk across a shaky bridge with a male or female experimenter at the end of the bridge. The shakiness of the bridge caused arousal and after the participant got to the end of the bridge the experimenters would pass them a questionnaire with their phone number on it. The idea being that when the experimenter was a female the male would transfer their excitement; the arousal; to the female and be more likely to call the female experimenter than the male experimenter. The results confirmed this idea and the effect is called Excitation Transfer.

Overall, showing you that emotion can be indirect as in this study the emotion wasn't caused by the female experimenter. It was caused by the shaky bridge.

Equally, an example from my own life where this happened is that most of the people who I have been sexually interested in I have felt strong feelings for them caused by their physical attractiveness and personality. This is an example of direct emotions.

Whereas, my friendships; which are classed as relationships; have been caused by both direct and indirect feelings. For example, one friendship that I had that was caused by people talking about them positively so by the time I met them. I already liked them so after we got talking. We quickly became friends.

I know that this is a mixture of direct and indirect feelings, but I still strongly believe that the indirect feelings helped the friendship to form.

<u>Attitudes and Similarity:</u>

In relationships, the similarity of attitudes, interests and values are important.

If you think about it you'll probably find that you, your partner and friends, past partners as well as friends or people that you would like to have a relationship will probably have similar attitudes.

For instance: I and my friend had many similar

attitudes towards certain things. Some of our similar attitudes included opinions of certain people, favourite food, world views, self-views and many more.

In fact, Galton (1970, 1952) found that wives and husbands are more similar than would occur via chance.

Therefore, supporting the idea that people in relationships are drawn together due to their similarity in attitudes.

What do you think?

Additionally, Festinger (1964) states that taking part in social comparison; where we compare each other to others; in relationships is one way to validate our own attitudes and beliefs. (See Sociocultural Psychology for more information)

We do this in relationships to make ourselves feel good.

We all have done this sort of comparison to our friends, family or loved ones.

I have done this before when I used to compare myself to one of my friends in terms of their quality of friendships and the quantity that they had as they seem to have more friends than myself.

However, I forget that I had what I needed. I

had friends and that was what I needed.

Thus, showing how we compare ourselves with people we are in relationships with.

(I'll explain this concept more as well as the pros and cons of social comparison in Sociocultural psychology)

Going back to similarity, sometimes we seek or prefer complementary personalities, values or other things instead of similarities.

<u>For Example:</u>

A serious person might like to have a funny person around.

A very liberal person might like to have a more conservative person around.

A risk-taker might like to have someone who is more risk aversive around to keep them grounded.

A personal example of this in my own life is that a past friendship involved myself and another boy who was the perfect complement to myself as we still had a lot in common but we both had different complimenting characteristics. Such as I thought things through and he didn't, he was very fun whilst I was only fun and more.

Overall, complementary characteristics can lead

to liking yet in general, birds of a feather flock together.

Nonetheless going back to my friend, a lot of people thought that we will complete opposites so they couldn't understand why we were such great friends. This brings us to another interesting piece of psychological knowledge, where people can appear opposite but in fact, they can be similar in fundamental ways.

For me and my friend, we were fundamentally the same when it came to our thoughts on people, the world and other matters that we both deemed as important.

On the other hand, complementary characteristics are especially important in relationships that are a 'fling' but these relationships don't last long.

Reciprocity Principle:

Finally, an important cognitive reason for why relationships form is the reciprocity principle. This is where we like people who like us.

This I think we can all say is generally true as most of our friendships started because we liked another person. Subsequently, you'll probably find that because you liked them. This probably led to them like you. Thus, forming a relationship or forming some sort of foundation, at least.

Hopefully, you are more interested in the psychology of human relationships. I personally do find it interesting because there is still a long way to go in terms of understanding, but we've made a good start.

More information psychology human relationship please check out [The Psychology of Human Relationships 2nd Edition.](#)

CHAPTER 7: HEALTH PSYCHOLOGY

Originally, I believe that health psychology was an extremely dry subfield of psychology because I was ignorant about what health psychology involved.

Therefore, I decided to write my Health Psychology book to explore at Health Psychology in more depth.

My research showed me that Health Psychology was fascinating because Health Psychology looks at how psychological, biological and social factors can cause and impact physical health.

In addition, my research into health psychology revealed to me one of my absolutely psychological models: The Biopsychosocial Model.

Personally, I love this model because this model as it focuses on the interaction between biological, cognitive and social factors to give you a behaviour. The reason why I love this model is because I am a great believer in holistic psychology. This means that I prefer to focus on the whole picture of behaviour instead of trying to narrow down the cause of a disorder or health problem to one cause.

Consequently, the biopsychosocial model looks at obesity in a number of ways because instead of looking at the hormonal reason, mindset reason as well as the fast-food cultural reason. The model combines these factors to give us one holistic reason or series of reasons for why obesity develops.

The opposite of holism is reduction.

Below is a sample chapter from [Health Psychology](#) that looks at the Biopsychosocial Model in more depth.

Chapter 2: The Biopsychosocial Model Of Health And Well-Being

I do truly love this approach to treatment because I believe that if you focus on a problem using only one approach; biological, cognitive or sociocultural; then your research could be heavily flawed and futile as you are trying to find one cause of the problem without considering the other causes.

In addition, in the real-world things are never as clear cut as we want them to be.

For example: later in the book we'll be looking at

the causes of obesity and as I'll show you there is no one cause of obesity. It's caused by a mixture of biological, cognitive and sociocultural factors.

As a result of this treatment should focus on the interaction of the three approaches as well.

The Biopsychosocial (BPS) model focuses on how biological, cognitive and social factors interact to develop into a disease.

For example, the BPS model looks at family relationships as a way to explain how a disease could develop as it involves psychological and social factors.

You will begin to understand as well as see examples of the BPS model being used through the book.

Yet for now, think of it as bringing together biological, cognitive and social factors to produce a holistic view of a health problem.

Nguyen et al (2016)

142 patient took part in a holistic weight loss programme that included: knowledge of insulin and its role in storing fat in the body, cognitive behavioural therapy to reframe thinking about food and behavioural therapy. To break unhealthy eating habits.

In addition, a drug called: Phentermine was

prescribed as well as the other two types of therapy.

Then the participants followed an eating schedule for 5 days a week and they were told never to starve themselves, but to avoid sweets as well as artificial sweeteners.

Results, shown that there was an average decrease in weight of 10.8% from the baseline to the end of the 86-day programme, and BMI decreased from 34.6 to 30.1.

In conclusion, this holistic approach to weight loss may be more effective to other weight loss programmes as they only tend to focus on one or two aspects of the BPS model.

Critical Thinking:

While this study uses a large sample size to create more data for them to support their conclusions. Making the study more reliability.

The study doesn't use another diet or weight loss group that only focuses on one or two aspects of the BPS model. This would make the findings more reliability as we could directly compare the holistic approach to obesity and the other types of programmes that only focus on one or two aspects of the model. Overall, allowing us to see which approach is best or how much of a difference this holistic approach makes.

Summary:

The BPS model focuses on the interaction of biological, cognitive and social factors.

Nguyen et al (2016) demonstrated that a holistic approach to treatment could be more effective than focusing on only two aspects of the BPS model.

For more information on how health psychology can impact obesity including its biological, cognitive and social factors as well as more about health psychology in general, please check out Health Psychology.

CHAPTER 8: DEVELOPMENTAL PSYCHOLOGY

Back in Autumn/Winter 2018, I remember talking to my psychology teacher at the time and we were discussing developmental psychology.

Basically, we were saying how dry the topic was as well as I remember saying that developmental psychology was basically done.

Of course, I look back on that conservation and laugh at myself- because this was before I wrote my developmental psychology book as well as before I went to University.

If I had the same conservation now, then I would say that developmental psychology is definitely not something I would go into for a job because you're researching children.

However, developmental psychology is great due

to it teaches you how children develop as well as it explains a lot of child behaviour that I didn't know the reason for.

Another reason why developmental psychology is very good is because of the breath than this type of psychology covers.

For example, developmental psychology covers:

- Brain development
- Cognitive development
- Effects of poverty on development
- How peers affect our development
- Attachment
- Gender identity
- And many more areas…

In other words, developmental psychology covers everything to do with how a child develops.

One of my favourite topics of developmental psychology is the effects of poverty on child development so below is an extract from Developmental Psychology.

Chapter 8: Poverty

Poverty is the state of having no or little means to fulfil basic needs and as a result of that, a number of outcomes can arise that inhibit development.

Brooks and Dunn (1997) summarised that poverty has a number of key outcomes:

- Physical health as poverty leads to stunted growth, malnourish and low birth weight.
- Lower cognitive ability
- Poorer school achievement
- Emotional as well as behavioural outcomes such as showing more aggression or fighting behaviour while feeling depressed or anxious on the inside.

The researchers suggested a number of pathways as well. These pathways are other factors that affect development in addition to the family income.

- Availability of nutrition
- The physical condition of the home
- Amount of time parents spent with children
- Parenting style
- Punishment practices
- Parent's mental health
- Neighbour conditions
- And many more…

<u>Models of Poverty:</u>

There are two main models or theories that try to explain and predict the deciding factors in the argument of what factors affect development the most.

The family stress theory states that the main variables that affect development are family-related. Like: parenting styles and communication strategies.

The investment model states that the most important pathways that affect development are associated with real goods. Such as nutrition, opportunities to learn and enriched environments.

Personally, if you combine the two theories, I believe that you would be spot on and both are very true explanations to the factors that affect poverty the most.

Pollitt (1995)

Researchers carried out a study on four very poor villages in Central Guatemala for the course of 8 years.

The participants were made up of over 2000 children and mothers.

As protein was the main nutrient missing from the villager's diet. The villagers were given a nutrient supplement.

Participant from two villages received a high protein supplement whereas the two other control villages got a supplement that contained far less protein.

Results showed that a significant drop in infant

mortality in both sets of villages, but with a 69% decrease in villages taking the high protein supplement compared to only a 24% decrease in the other two villages. Children on the lower protein supplement suffered a slower rate of growth and a slower rate of recovery from infection. They also learned to crawl and walk slightly later on average. Because these undernourished children remained small for their age, adults may have treated them as if they were younger than their actual age.

In conclusion, this shows how poverty can affect psychological development.

Critical Thinking:

A positive of this study is that it has high ecological validity as the experiment uses a natural, real-world setting. In turn, this increases the generalizability of the findings, so we apply the results of the experiment to different situations.

However, as a result of this high ecological validity where other factors that could influence cognitive development aren't controlled. We cannot say with unshakable certainty that protein was the only factor that could have given us these results. As factors could have potentially played a role. Like: illness, genetic factors and other missing nutrients from their diet.

Summary:

Poverty can have a number of impacts on development.

There are a number of factors that impact development as well as family income.

The two main theories or models in relation to the effects of poverty on development are:

The family stress theory

The investment model

Pollitt (1995) demonstrated how important protein is in cognitive development.

After reading that chapter, I hope that you can see that poverty has a massive effect on child development.

However, it must be remembered that a lot of more other factors can impact human development as well. For instance, brain development, cognitive development and even playing with others.

For more information on child development, please check out Developmental Psychology.

CHAPTER 9: RESEARCH IN PSYCHOLOGY

What makes good research?

How do you research human behaviour?

What problems do psychological researchers face?

These are vital questions in psychology because if we aren't able to research human behaviour effectively then psychology WILL become a false-science as psychological 'facts' will supported by nothing except opinions as well as weak evidence.

In all honesty, this chapter is very difficult to write because I want to be helpful but without putting the entire book of Research In Psychology inside this book. it's very difficult to tell you what makes good research.

However, the sample chapter below will

hopefully serve as a good introduction for you so you can understand how research is conducted within psychology.

Chapter 1: Research Types

In psychological research, there are two types of research.

<u>Quantitative:</u>

The aim of this research is to make universal rules of behaviour. That can be applied to a large group of people.

The focus is on how behaviour is created and shows itself with a strong emphasis on scientific number-based data.

Furthermore, it's an objective type of research meaning that the researcher is removed from the research context and doesn't influence the results as much.

Some examples of this type of research include:

- Experiments
- Natural experiments
- Correlational studies

Overall, think of this type of research as the hardcore type of science that is supported by hard facts and numerical data.

Qualitative research:

The aim of this type is to develop a deep understanding of a particular event or case. As a result of this focus on one event, this type of research doesn't produce universal rules of behaviour.

Qualitative research focuses on human experiences, interpretation and meaning with rich detailed texts for data.

However, this type is less objective as the researcher is part of the research method and could possibly influence the results.

Some qualitative methods include:

- Case studies
- Observations
- Focus groups
- Interviews

Overall, think as this type of research as focusing one event and trying to find out everything about the event. In order to write a very, very detailed report of why the event happened.

I hope that you have found this useful and for more information on research, please check out Research in Psychology.

WHAT IS PSYCHOLOGY?

CHAPTER 10: FORENSIC PSYCHOLOGY

Personally, this is one of those times when something that has already been written is better than I could explain it now.

Therefore, below a chapter from Forensic Psychology that details what Forensic Psychology involves, as well as I love Forensic Psychology so I truly hope that you find this interesting.

Introduction: What Is Forensic Psychology?
Forensic Psychology is honestly one of my favourite types of psychology because I love the criminal mind and crime-related behaviour.

However, I must confer that forensic psychology is not profiling or what we typically see on television programmes. Such as CSI, NCIS or Bones.

In this chapter, we will be exploring what forensic psychology involves before we explore the various topics of forensic psychology.

What is Forensic Psychology?

This is a difficult question as there is no one answer.

Forensic psychology could be defined in many ways including:

- The psychological study of crime.
- The scientific behavioural study criminals.
- The science of studying crime-related behaviour.

I think we can all agree that these definitions are okay and do describe what we know as forensic psychology, but they are all wrong or not as good as they could be.

For example, the first definition states that we only study crime but forensic psychology studies more than crime.

The second definition has the same problem as it states that we only study criminals.

Finally, the third definition is a bit ambiguous as forensic psychology does study crime-related incidents, but this definition possibly sounds as if forensic psychology studies everything but the crime itself.

Consequently, what is forensic psychology?

We can define forensic psychology as the activities of all psychologists whose work is related or contributes to the criminal justice system.

I know that this sounds complicated, but I'll explain it in the next section.

The Autonomy of Forensic Psychology

Is forensic psychology autonomous of other fields of psychology?

I ask you this question because other fields of psychology are quite autonomous, yet no subfield can be completely autonomous; as biological psychology is relatively autonomous as it studies biological processes and behaviour, so it doesn't draw very much information from other subfields. Like: cognitive psychology that focuses on mental processes.

The answer to the question is no.

Forensic psychology is not an autonomous subfield as psychological areas that are related to forensic psychology include but are not limited to:

- Social psychology- it's important to understand how the psychological processes within groups impact crime.

- Clinical psychology- it's important to understand as mental disorders impact or relate to criminal behaviour.
- Cognitive psychology- it's important to know how a person's mental processes can cause them to commit a crime.
- Developmental psychology- it's important to know how child development can cause crime.
- Personality- how a person's personality increases their likelihood to commit a crime.

Overall, as you can see forensic psychology works with and draws on the knowledge of other fields to help us understand crime and crime-related behaviour.

Forensic Psychology As A Field:

Forensic psychology is a very unique field within psychology as within most fields you can either be a researcher; so you research behaviour; or you can be a practitioner; where you apply the research to the real world in treatment or other settings; so you cannot be both.

However, in forensic psychology, you can be both.

This career opportunity is very interesting as there is often conflict between practitioners as well as researchers. As a result, the researchers do not write the reports or research in a practical way or a way that the practitioners can use. Making it very difficult to apply the research that could be extremely beneficial to offenders on treatment programmes in a treatment setting.

Overall, forensic psychology is an amalgamation of psychological work and practices.

In addition, forensic psychology is a fast-evolving area which holds many national and international conferences to keep everyone updated.

Some of These Conferences Include:

- The British Psychology Society Division of Forensic Psychology Annual Meeting
- International Association for Correctional and Forensic Psychology

Where Can You Work As A Forensic Psychologist?

Forensic psychology offers a lot of different work opportunities for you including:

- Treating offenders in a public or private prison
- Treating offenders in hospitals or other clinical settings
- Carrying out assessments on offenders. These assessments can possibly include suicide risk assessment and clinical assessments.

- Research- which is covered in the next section
- Consultancy

Even within the research side of forensic psychology, there are a lot of options for you.

For instance, you could research:

- Gangs- what causes them?
- Sexual aggression- why do some people commit sexual offenders and others do not?
- Firesetting- why are more males arsonists compared to females?
- Violence- what social causes provoke aggression?
- Child abuse- why abuse children?
- Terrorism- what causes terrorists to commit acts of mass murder?

All these areas of research involve both basic research; where you just research the fundamental variables, which is typically done in labs; and applied research. This is where you use the research in the real world.

Ethics within Forensic Psychology:

'Beware the actions of man.

Beware the lust for power and knowledge.

Beware the morality and ethics of a man'

-Connor Whiteley

Whilst I say that quote jokingly, it is no less true as ethics is a major part of psychology and the ethical guidelines were bought into creation by Man's questionable and *evil* actions as their lust for power as well as knowledge made them do harsh and unethical things to people.

For example: in the Stanford Prison Experiments in its oversimplified form where the researchers placed people in a situation without oversight to see what people would do as they wanted the knowledge to understand human behaviour further. Resulting in the unethical treatment of the people in the prisoner condition.

Please check out Sociocultural Psychology for more information.

Linking to forensic psychology, ethics can impact our ability to study criminal behaviour for a few reasons.

For example, we cannot study rape in a natural setting as this would be extremely unethical as we would effectively be watching a rapist rape a person and allowing it to happen for the sole purpose of gathering data. Whilst, the rape victim's life was destroyed.

That was one extreme example.

A less extreme example would be if researchers joined a gang and carried out drug deals (illegal behaviour) in order to gather data on drug users and the world of narcotics.

Therefore, as you can see ethics can inhibit forensic psychological research.

How Can Forensic Psychology Help The Progression Of Justice?

Forensic psychology can be extremely useful in the quest for justice, but with all disciplines. Forensic Psychology does have its limitations. This will be explored later in this book.

Some ways that Forensic Psychology can help the progression of justice include:

- It can improve eyewitness testimony.
- It can inform police procedure. For instance, by giving them more reliable ways to improve suspect identification.
- It can reveal what is involved in crime.
- It can inform treatments for offenders.

Attitudes and Philosophical Perspectives to have in Forensic Psychology:

Whilst, this section is more aimed at students of forensic psychology, I still strongly believe that this will be useful throughout this book as together we will have to be critical of research in Forensic Psychology.

Therefore, within Forensic Psychology (and wider psychology) it's important to bear the following in mind:

- You need to be analytical and critical.
- Don't use common sense has this causes too many problems and it often isn't correct.
- You should be sceptical but not cynical.
- You need to remember that crime has a context. For example, a mother killing the man who slaughtered her daughter is different from a woman who killed her boyfriend because he was going to leave her. Despite them both being murders.
- You need to examine theories as well as beliefs scientifically.
- When you try to understand or explain a crime, you need to consider both situational factors; like a poor neighbour, abusive parents and having children; and individual factors. Like: intelligence and abnormal sexual arousal.

History of Forensic Psychology:

Forensic Psychology in the early 1900s had great interest before it died and picked up in the 1970s again.

However, Forensic Psychology can be traced

back centuries as the concepts of insanity and fitness to stand trial are centuries old.

Forensic Psychology has developed an infrastructure to encourage its continued existence through international conferences, publications and journals.

Now that we have a basic understanding of what Forensic Psychology is, we can now start to explore the various topics within Forensic Psychology in more depth…

On a quick parting note, Forensic Psychology is a fascinating area to read about and I loved writing my book as I got to learn about sexual offending, theories of offending, rehabilitation, treatment and some other VERY surprising facts.

So in the event that you do want to know more about Forensic Psychology, please check out my book Forensic Psychology.

PARTING NOTE:

As a result of this book, I truly hope that you have discovered something new about psychology and human behaviour because I love psychology and the whole point of these books and me being a psychology author is to help people.

In addition, even if you don't go onto the rest of my psychology book series, I hope that you've learned something.

I wish you all the best in your future psychological endeavours.

BIBLIOGRAPHY:

Flangan, C, Hartnoll, L, Murray, R (2015) Psychology A Level and AS Level Book 1, Oxford University Press

Whiteley, C (2019) Biological Psychology, CGD Publishing

Whiteley, C (2019) Cognitive Psychology, CGD Publishing

Whiteley, C (2020) Sociocultural Psychology, 2nd Edition, CGD Publishing

Whiteley, C (2019) Abnormal Psychology, CGD Publishing

Whiteley, C (2020) The Psychology of Human Relationships, 2nd Edition, CGD Publishing

Whiteley, C (2019) Health Psychology, CGD Publishing

Whiteley, C (2019) Developmental Psychology, CGD Publishing

Whiteley, C (2019) Research in Psychology, CGD Publishing

Whiteley, C (2020) Forensic Psychology, CGD Publishing

https://www.subscribepage.com/psychologyboxset

Thank you for reading.

I hoped you enjoyed it.

If you want a FREE book and keep up to date about new books and project. Then please sign up for my newsletter at www.connorwhiteley.net/

Have a great day.

CHECK OUT THE PSYCHOLOGY WORLD PODCAST FOR MORE PSYCHOLOGY INFORMATION!

AVAILABLE ON ALL MAJOR PODCAST APPS.

About the author:

Connor Whiteley is the author of over 30 books in the sci-fi fantasy, nonfiction psychology and books for writer's genre and he is a Human Branding Speaker and Consultant.

He is a passionate warhammer 40,000 reader, psychology student and author.

Who narrates his own audiobooks and he hosts The Psychology World Podcast.

All whilst studying Psychology at the University of Kent, England.

Also, he was a former Explorer Scout where he gave a speech to the Maltese President in August 2018 and he attended Prince Charles' 70th Birthday Party at Buckingham Palace in May 2018.

Plus, he is a self-confessed coffee lover!

Please follow me on:

Website: www.connorwhiteley.net

Twitter: @scifiwhiteley

Please leave on honest review as this helps with the discoverability of the book and I truly appreciate it.

Thank you for reading. I hope you've enjoyed.

All books in 'An Introductory Series':

BIOLOGICAL PSYCHOLOGY 3RD EDITION

COGNITIVE PSYCHOLOGY 2ND EDITION

SOCIAL PSYCHOLOGY- 3RD EDITION

ABNORMAL PSYCHOLOGY 3RD EDITION

PSYCHOLOGY OF RELATIONSHIPS- 3RD EDITION

DEVELOPMENTAL PSYCHOLOGY 3RD EDITION

HEALTH PSYCHOLOGY

RESEARCH IN PSYCHOLOGY

A GUIDE TO MENTAL HEALTH AND TREATMENT AROUND THE WORLD- A GLOBAL LOOK AT DEPRESSION

FORENSIC PSYCHOLOGY

CLINICAL PSYCHOLOGY

FORMULATION IN PSYCHOTHERAPY

Other books by Connor Whiteley:

THE ANGEL OF RETURN

THE ANGEL OF FREEDOM

GARRO: GALAXY'S END

GARRO: RISE OF THE ORDER

GARRO: END TIMES

GARRO: SHORT STORIES

GARRO: COLLECTION

GARRO: HERESY

GARRO: FAITHLESS

GARRO: DESTROYER OF WORLDS

GARRO: COLLECTIONS BOOK 4-6

GARRO: MISTRESS OF BLOOD

GARRO: BEACON OF HOPE

GARRO: END OF DAYS

WINTER'S COMING

WINTER'S HUNT

WINTER'S REVENGE

WINTER'S DISSENSION

Companion guides:

BIOLOGICAL PSYCHOLOGY 2ND EDITION WORKBOOK

COGNITIVE PSYCHOLOGY 2ND EDITION WORKBOOK

SOCIOCULTURAL PSYCHOLOGY 2ND EDITION WORKBOOK

ABNORMAL PSYCHOLOGY 2ND EDITION WORKBOOK

PSYCHOLOGY OF HUMAN RELATIONSHIPS 2ND EDITION WORKBOOK

HEALTH PSYCHOLOGY WORKBOOK

FORENSIC PSYCHOLOGY WORKBOOK

Audiobooks by Connor Whiteley:

BIOLOGICAL PSYCHOLOGY

COGNITIVE PSYCHOLOGY

SOCIOCULTURAL PSYCHOLOGY

ABNORMAL PSYCHOLOGY

PSYCHOLOGY OF HUMAN RELATIONSHIPS

HEALTH PSYCHOLOGY

DEVELOPMENTAL PSYCHOLOGY

RESEARCH IN PSYCHOLOGY

FORENSIC PSYCHOLOGY

GARRO: GALAXY'S END

GARRO: RISE OF THE ORDER

GARRO: SHORT STORIES

GARRO: END TIMES

GARRO: COLLECTION

GARRO: HERESY

GARRO: FAITHLESS

GARRO: DESTROYER OF WORLDS

GARRO: COLLECTION BOOKS 4-6

GARRO: COLLECTION BOOKS 1-6

Business books:

TIME MANAGEMENT: A GUIDE FOR STUDENTS AND WORKERS

LEADERSHIP: WHAT MAKES A GOOD LEADER? A GUIDE FOR STUDENTS AND WORKERS.

BUSINESS SKILLS: HOW TO SURVIVE THE BUSINESS WORLD? A GUIDE FOR STUDENTS, EMPLOYEES AND EMPLOYERS.

BUSINESS COLLECTION

GET YOUR FREE BOOK AT:
WWW.CONNORWHITELEY.NET

Ingram Content Group UK Ltd.
Milton Keynes UK
UKHW021846100723
424887UK00006B/186